TERRA-COTTA WARRIORS AND HORSES AT THE TOMB OF QIN SHI HUANG,

THE FIRST EMPEROR OF CHINA

Compiled by The Archaeological Team of Pit of
Terra-cotta Figures at Qin Shi Huang Mausoleum
and The Museum of Qin Terra-cotta Figures

Cultural Relics Publishing House

Photo: Luo Zhongmin
Cover design: Qiu Dehu
Layout: Peng Huashi
Editors in charge: Shilan and Peng Huashi

First Edition. 1983
Fifth Printing, 1990

Compiled by
The Archaeological Team of Pit of Terra-cotta
Figures at Qin shi Huang Mausoleum and
The Museum of Qin Terra-cotta Figures
Published and Distributed by the Cultural Relics Publishing House
29, Wusi Dajie, Beijing, China

Printed by Beijing No.2 Offset Printing Factory
Printed in the People's Republic of China

ISBN7-5010-0141-3/K·52 （外）

CONTENTS

Terra-cotta Warriors in Armour and Horses
at the Tomb of Qin Shi Huang

by Yuan Zhongyi

The tumulus of Qin Shi Huang (China's first emperor) containing terra cotta warriors in armour and horses consists of the No. 1, No. 2, and No. 3 pits. The huge grave complex lay in the east of the actual tomb of the emperor. Since 1974 explorations and trial excavations were carried out, from which a basic knowledge of the formation and content of the pits had been obtained. Its scale is magnificent; it has an area of over 20,000 square metres. It forms a rich treasure house of China's cultural relics or historical monuments. Twenty wooden war chariots, more than a thousand life-size terra cotta warriors in armour and horses, plus 10,000 odd bronze weapons had been unearthed during the trial excavation. Judging from what had been revealed so far there are 100 odd war chariots, 600 odd clay horses and over 7,000 terra cotta warriors, and a massive quantity of real weaponry.

The wariors and horses are arranged in ancient Chinese battle formation. In the No. 1 pit are found war chariots and foot soldiers arrayed in rectangle. Chariots, cavalry and infantry form a curve in the No. 2 pit. While in the No. 3 pit terra cotta warriors line the route and guard the headquarters, which commands the army found in the preceding two pits. They are all life-size pottery figures, the once powerful army of the State of Qin in miniature. They are vivid material objects for a study of the military equipment, army establishment, and battle formation of the State of Qin. The life-like figures of warriors possess distinct characters and features. Simple in style, they possess rich artistic appeal, symbolising the consumation of the art of ancient Chinese sculpture. They serve as a link between the past and the present.

The magnificent discovery of the terra cotta figures of warriors in armour and horses has made itself the focuss of world attention. It is now regarded as another wonder of the world and a treasure house of ancient spiritual civilisation of mankind.

I. General Description of Three Pits Containing
Terra Cotta Figures of Qin Warriors

The three pits, in which were buried terra cotta figures of warriors and horses of Qin Shi Huang, lie east of the ancient tumulus of China's first emperor, at a distance of 1.5 kilometres. It is to the north of the grand path leading to the eastern gate of the royal sepulcher. The warriors and horses are a sacrifice to the dead emperor.

In March, 1974 members of the Xiyang Village, Yanzhai Rural Commune, Lintong County, Shaanxi Province made their first discovery of No. 1 pit while digging a well.

Archaeologists in the province rushed to the scene. During the trial excavation information was obtained about the size of the pit and the relics that lay buried underneath. In the summer of 1976 the No. 2 and No. 3 pits were discovered to the north of the first pit, 20-25 metres away. (Still another pit was discovered at a point between the No. 2 and No. 3 pits. It was empty and nothing was found there. The empty pit is usually not included in the grave complex by archaeologists. Following exploration and trial digging the three pits were found to contain rich cultural relics housed on great scale. The terra cotta figures of warriors and horses stand about the size of real men and real horses. The discovery is indeed a great one in the history of Chinese archaeology. A huge sum was allocated by the Chinese people's government to be used for the building of a big exhibition hall, 230 metres long, 22 metres wide and with a span of 72 metres — over an area of 16,000 square metres. The hall now covers the pit in its entirety.

The No. 2 and No. 3 pits have now been refilled, after the trial excavation. About 1,000 pottery warriors and horses excavated in the No. 2 pit, after due repair, are now arrayed in their original stance. The rows and rows of towering warriors and horses show distinct features, great and extraordinary, giving one the atmosphere of magnitude and power in their bearing.

1. Building Structure of Pits

The No. 1, No. 2 and No. 3 pits all contain structures of earth and wood in subterranean galleries. The No. 1 and No. 2 pits had been burnt as a result of fire and collapsed. The No. 3 pit also caved-in due to natural decay of wooden canopy. However, before collapse it was seriously damaged by the army of General Xiang Yu upon entering into the gateway Tongguan Pass guarding China proper. The buildings on the ground level were burnt, leaving behind heaps of debris, in which broken tiles, ashes and scorched earth can still be seen today. Historians infer that the pits could have been looted and burnt by General Xiang Yu, who, it was said, also burnt palaces built by the first emperor.

The No. 1 pit is a rectangle running from east to west. The length from the east end to the west end is 230 metres while the breadth (from south to north) is 62 metres. There are five slanting covered passages on both ends of east and west and both sides of north and south. The covered passages on the two ends (east and west) of the pit are 15-20 meters long and 3.8-6.6 meters wide. The covered passages on the sides south and north are a bit smaller — 12 meters long and 1.6-4.8 meters wide. These are apparently side doors. Positioned in the west the pit faces east. The door on the east is the main entrance. On entering into the main entrance one sees two long corridors, 60 meters long (from south to north) and 3.45 meters wide on both the east and west ends of the pit. There is a side corridor on the south and north ends of the pit, each measuring 180 meters long and 2 meters wide.

Sandwiched in between these corridors are nine tunnels (each 180 meters long and 3.5 meters wide), which are separated by walls of rammed earth. On the corridors are arrayed terra cotta foot soldiers. In the tunnels are chariots and foot soldiers alongside each other.

The No. 2 pit is at the northern side of the east end of No. 1 pit. The two pits are only 20 meters apart. The plane figure of the pit is like a carpenter's square. The length, at the east and west, is 124 meters at the most and the width (from north to south) is 98 meters at the most. The measurement includes covered passages at the entrance. The depth of the pit is five meters. The area is 6,000 square meters.

There are three slanting covered passages on the east and west sides, but only one on the north side. The structure of the interior, based on the different arms of services, is largely divided into four units. Unit 1 is situated at the northeast corner, or the extreme end of the curve. The plane figure looks like a square (26.6 × 38 meters). The four sides are surrounded by corridors, each 3.2 meters wide. In the middle are four tunnels running east to west. Archers with crossbows stand in the long corridor. In the tunnels are archers with crossbows, bending on knees. Unit 2 is situated half way to the right. The plane figure resembles a square, 52 × 48 meters. A long corridor, south to north, can be found on the east and west sides of the unit. Eight tunnels, east to west, are in the center. Warriors are absent in the long corridors. Chariots in square battle position are in the tunnels. Unit 3, in the center of the pit, forms itself into a rectangle as a plane figure (86 × 16 meter). On the east end a wall made of rammed earth separates unit 3 from unit 1. On the wall is an open door to allow passage. On the west end is a side corridor, with three tunnels, east to west. In the tunnels are chariots, foot soldiers, and cavalry in rectangle battle position. Unit 4 is on the left side of the pit; its plane figure also looks like a rectangle (50 × 20 meters). The eastern end is separated from Unit 1 by a wall with an open door. A side corridor is to the west side. There are three tunnels, running east to west, in the middle. Cavalry form into a rectangle in the tunnels. The four are comparatively speaking independent units. Yet they combine to form into a strictly integrated whole as well.

No. 3 pit lies to the north of the west end of No. 1 pit. The two are 25 meters apart. The plane figure of No. 3 pit look like a concave, 17.6 metres long (from east to west), 21.4 meters wide (from south to north), and 4.8 meters deep. The area is 520 square meters. Rather odd looking, the structure of the pit is a bit complicated. On the east a slanting covered passage leads to the pit. Entering the door one finds a stable, in which stands a chariot. Two long corridors, on the left and right sides of the stable, are connected with two chambers. The southern chamber is made up of an antechamber, a back chamber, and a corridor. The northern chamber is a rectangle (8 × 4 meters) running from east to west. At the entrance of this chamber and the northern exit of the long corridor are four brass rings with handles, equidistant from each other. This provides a clue that there must have been drapes originally. Sixty four warriors line up the route in the northern chamber. They wield bronze poles, which are ancient weapons. They look like imperial guards. No. 3 pit is the army headquarters.

The construction of the subterranean vaults is like this: the three pits were dug, five meters deep, according to shape. Rammed earth walls were erected on four sides of the pits. Tunnels were dug in the middle. Between tunnels partition walls were erected. Wooden pillars were made to stand, 1.4 meters apart, on left and right hand sides of the surroundings of the pit as well as that of the partition walls. The bottom of the pillar was buttressed by rectangle wood. The upper part were roof timber horizontal supports. The wooden trellis was thus formed, very much like the framework above Chinese wells for drawing water. On the trellis and the top of partition walls were arranged rows and rows of wood as ceiling, covered with mat, either made of clay, red soil, or loese. This formed the roof, two meters above ground. The floor was paved with green bricks. The space from the bricked floor to the roof is 3.2-3.8 meters. The terra cotta warriors and horses were now left in the pit. The covered passages were sealed with wood, to be left standing. Once this was done the whole structure became a sealed, magnificent subterranean architecture.

The barracks of ancient Chinese army was called bi lei or military breast-work. The No. 1 pit can be regarded as the bi lei or the army on the right whereas the No. 2 pit that of the army on the left. No. 3 pit in the center is the headquarters. The army establishment in ancient China is divided in the same way, as a rule. The only thing missing, however, is the main army in the center. The unfinished pit north of the center of No. 1 pit, halfway between No. 2 and No. 3 pits, has an area of 4,608 square meters (96 × 48 meters). It could well be where the central army was supposed to be. The pit is now filled with sand. There are no traces of bricks, wooden structures or pottery soldiers. The reason is that the peasant army in rebellion led by Zhou Zhang approached the River Xi at the northern foot of Mount Li in 209 B.C., which called a halt to the construction of the first emperor's tomb.

The grave complex of subterranean vaults, biggest in scale, is seldom seen in the history of archaeology, Chinese or foreign. They occupy a total of 25,388 square meters of floor space. The earth removed from the pit reached 100,000 odd cubic meters. The wood used are all huge pines and cypresses. From the wooden trough visible the diameter of the wood used for the ceiling is 68 cm. The tallest wood reaches 10 odd meters.

According to preliminary estimate a total of 8,000 odd cubic meters of wood had been used in the three pits. Reed or bamboo mat covering the ceiling reached a total of 18,000 cubic meters. Bricks used to pave the floor totalled 250,000. On top of this 7,000 terra cotta warriors and horses had to be made. The project must have involved a tremendous amount of manpower and money.

Such subterranean vaults could not have been constructed in a short period of time. When was the project begun: How long did it actually take? The answers to these questions are unfortunately not given in written Chinese history. The inscriptions on unearthed weapons indicate that the earliest were dated the 3rd year of the reign of Qin Shi Huang while the latest was dated the 19th year. The weapons couldn't have been buried earlier than 19th year (228 B.C.). This was seven years before the first emperor unified the six warring states or the 26th year of his reign (221 B.C.). *Shi Ji* or "Historical Records" says that 700,000 persons were pressed into service for the construction of the grave during the early years of the ascension to the throne of the first emperor. From this it can be deduced that construction must have begun after China became a unified country. The construction of pits of terra cotta warriors was likely to have begun at the same time until it was halted in 209 B.C. A total of 10 years must have been spent for the entire project.

In the refill of No. 1 pit workers' iron chops and iron spades had been discovered. At the southern side of No. 1 pit what looked like the remains of large sheds — once the living quarters of construction workers, had also been unearthed. Many convicts must have been employed to dig the pits. From the inscriptions on the terra cotta figures it can be seen that many pottery workers must have been employed to mould and smelt the pottery figures. People of such low and humble position are actually the creators of the Qin terra cotta figures of warriors in the pits.

4

2. The Position of Pits Housing Terra Cotta Figures of Warriors in the First Emperor's Royal Sepulchere

The emperor's grave lies at the southern foot of Mount Li. To the north is the River Wei. From a distance the royal grave looks like a towering hill. The grave used to be 115 meters high. Its base is 485 × 515 meters (from east to west and from south to north). The area is 249,775 sq. meters. Due to corrosion by rain and water as well as man's own destruction the grave is now reduced to 76 meters high, 345 meters long, and 350 meters wide. The area, too, is reduced to 20,750 sq. meters.

There are both inner and outer walls surrounding the grave. The walls, however, have now become dilapidated and collapsed. Only the base remains. As a result of exploration it has been discovered that both walled cities formed rectangles, from south to north. The inner walled city was 355 meters long (from south to north) and 580 meters wide (from east to west). The circumference was estimated at 3,870 meters. The outer walled city measured 2,165 meters long (from south to north) and 940 meters wide (from east to west). The circumference was 6,210 meters. City gates stood on four sides of both cities. The outer city had four gates on four sides, but the inner city only one gate each on east, west and south. There were two gates on the north side, however. Look out towers rose above the gates. The base of the tower above the south gate in inner city now still rises 2-3 meters above the surface of the earth. On the north and west sides of the grave mound what used to be old buildings today also remain above ground.

The underground architectures are on a far more grand scale than those above. On the west side of the grave mound two sets of huge bronze chariots and horses, all painted, have been unearthed. They are belived to be auxiliary vehicles for the ghost of the first emperor to ride during ghostly inspection tours. Between the inner and outer walled cities to the west of the royal tomb are 31 pits containing rare birds, rare animals as well as pottery soldiers, sitting or on knees. Skeletons of deers and other rare animals have been found alongside the pottery soldiers who are on knees. These have been unearthed objects so far. This means that it must be the royal garden. The first emperor had built many royal gardens, parks, towers, and pavilions. Flowers known for their beauty, rare fruits, rare birds, and odd looking animals were found in the gardens for the emperor to hunt or to enjoy. In the village of Shang Jiao Cun to the east of the outer wall 91 pits containing stables and pottery soldiers on knees were discovered. Test excavation in the winter of 1976 revealed 28 pits. In some pits the bones of a real horse were found. In others clay soldiers were found, in addition to the dead horses. Still others, however, contain one clay soldier only. These pits must be royal stables, and the terra cotta soldiers on knees were grooms, known as yu jen in ancient China.

Based on what has been excavated so far it seems that the royal sepulcher of the first emperor had been modelled on the palaces he lived during his lifetime. The underground sepulcher is a replica of the palaces that once stood on the ground.

Now what position do these three pits containing terra-cotta figures of warriors and horses assume in the entire underground palace? To get an answer to this question we must study the first emperor's Xian Yang Palace and Xian Yang city. Both had been guarded by troops. The garrison forces of the imperial city were roughly of three kinds:

5

(1) personal guards of the emperor, taken up by lang zhong. It was the duty of personal guards to guard palaces, and palace gates. When the emperor left the palace, the guards acted as cavalry to protect the royal carriage. The guards were under the command of lang zhong ling (head of the imperial guards).

(2) guards posted outside palace gates and commanded by wei wei.

(3) guards of the capital, recruited from cai shi of warring states conquered by the Qin.

The first two guards have not yet been discovered hitherto since the excavation is unfinished. But the three pits of terra cotta figures of warriors and horses on the north side of the main road leading to the eastern gate can be assumed to symbolise garrison troops outside the capital city. The three military guards were apparently used to protect the capital and to uphold the authority of the first emperor in eternity. Clearly this must have been the thinking behind the designing of the pits.

II. Models of War Chariots, Figures of Cavalry and Foot Soldiers Unearthed at the Tomb of the First Emperor of the Qin Dynasty

Twenty wooden chariots, one hundred odd terra cotta figures of horses drawing chariots, 29 saddled horses of the cavalry, 1,400 figures of warriors of various descriptions, and over 10,000 bronze weapons have been unearthed from the three pits so far after test excavations. It is estimated that at least a total of 130 odd chariots, over 500 clay horses that draw the vehicles, 116 saddled horses, and 7,000 men including those guarding the chariots, cavalry and foot soldiers could be buried in the pits. The vehicles, horses and soldiers are life size, arrayed in battle formation of ancient China. They are a symbolic record of the army of Qin.

1. Classification of Chariots, Cavalry and Foot Soldiers

(1) War chariots

They are of four kinds, classified according to different personnel and dresses.

a. Commanding chariots. The chariots are decorated in a luxurious manner with the entire body painted black. Geometric designs can be found on the chariot. The top is round, on which hang bell and drum. Three figures on the chariot are the general (on the left), the horse driver (in the middle), and an aide (on the right), whose job is to extricate the chariot when it is bogged down.

b. Auxiliary chariots. Two such chariots have been unearthed in the No. 2 pit. The chariot looks very much like the commanding chariot, only without the top and hanging bell and drum. A driver (in the middle) and an assistant (on the right) are seen. Usually there are three persons on a chariot. But two persons are seen on this type, which follows the chariot used by the general. The auxiliary chariot is seen at the head of the cavalry unit behind the commander of the cavalry.

ures are models of portraits of real persons. They are on a much larger scale and have attained a magnificence far exceeding all other clay figures. This is one of the reasons why the Qin Shi Huang's burial sacrifices have astounded the whole world.

This realism is at one with the style of the Qin period. Apart from the ensemble of huge clay sculptures, we find all sculptured art of the period having the same outstanding characteristic — huge and towering. After the first emperor unified the whole of China he collected all weapons in the country and had them cast into 12 gigantic bronze figures in Xian Yang. Standing before the emperor's palace, each giant weighs 240,000 catties. These bronze figures together with stone sculptures contain realism. As huge impressive objects they are an appendage to the grand palaces and mausoleum. It was said that the palaces of the Qin Dynasty towered high into sky, rising above hills and across valleys. They covered an area of 300 *li*. The mound of the royal tomb measures 50 *zhang* and the earth raised up extends well into five *li*. The whole atmosphere is grand, impressive and breath-taking. The style and imposing manner of the ensemble of huge figures in the underground vaults are quite similar to those of the Qin palaces. They complement each other in splendor.

Sculpture art as a superstructure ideology must be a reflection of the age in which it lives. In the Qin period the new emerging landlord class had ascended the stage of history. Much vigor had been witnessed in it. Qin Shi Huang as the political representative of his class, unified China and set up the Qin Dynasty. He regarded himself as a man whose merits had been unsurpassed by all previous rulers. He wanted to uphold his dignity, consolidate his rule over a unified country and establish his throne for all his descendants. To this end he introduced a serious of measures in political, economic, cultural, and artistic fields. He standardised the axle length of wagons and chariots, weights and measures as well as the system of writing Chinese characters. He codified the law and regulated moral relations. He also collected all weapons and even destroyed ramparts of city walls. In the field of architecture and art the aim was to achieve an effect whereby the emperor is seen as someone who is from heaven to govern the people down below. Led by this thinking the artists sculptured the image of the Qin army and represented its fighting spirit in sweeping away all enemies in the universe, conquering the Xiong Nu (nomadic people) in the north and pacifying the Bai Yue (southern minorities) in the south. As art the sculptures have epoch making significance. Such art can only have been created in the Qin Dynasty. In another word, it is a product of an age.

2. The Making of Images of Qin Figures

Though the Qin figures of warriors and so forth contain the characteristics of modelled portraits, yet the images produced are not naturalistic emulation of real persons and objects. They are artistic images having undergone refinement and condensation. The sculptors used a method to make figures that is simple, compendious and not overloaded with details. Attention is paid only to likeness of real persons and to the main features. In order to make the image vivid and life-like emphasis on certain parts of the body and artistic exaggerations have been given. The artist does not sculpture everything down to the minutest details but give prominence to such things as eyebrows, beard, which are made to look like something blowing or being blown upward. This exaggeration does not surprise the viewer nor gives an impression of lack of fidelity. The method, on the contrary, manifests the spirit and mettle of man, resulting in playing up individuality of character. There is a variety of hair style, such as screw style, fine-toothed style and wavy style. The sculptor made the hair into concaves and convexes very much like the hair seen on statues of buddhas in the case of screw style. For fine-toothed style the lines are a bit overlapping yet they look rather natural. The wavy style means the hair is sculptured unevenly and gives a strong impression very much like waves and dishevelled hair. The first two styles are highly adorned. The last emphasises on key effect, being bold and vigorous.

The braid has three strands or six. There is a variety of shapes, such as herring bone, cross, T-shaped or shaped like the Chinese character. There is a rich breath of life, too. The buns or coils look a bit formalised at a distance, but is actually highly variegated. They range from single deck bun, double deck ring, double ring, three rings, four-ring, three-deck single-ring, double-coil, three-coil, and four-coil. No one bun of hair has been arranged the same way. In sculpturing the bun the artist has combined decor in bas relief, round sculpture and engraving of lines into an integrated unit. The sculpture has unity and coherence. It gives a strong impression of quality. The strings used to bind the hair are either fan-like, wavy, curled or turned upward. They are in keeping with the system of ancient dress in China. Far from being dull looking, they contain rhyme and are rhythmetic. It shows that the sculptors have used with their deft hands the beauty of form into their art.

Qin sculptured models represent structure, quantity, shape, and quality of figures or objects. The artists have mastered the proportion of the human body and its structure. The robust body is matched with four strong limbs, a big head and wide face. A tall body is matched with long limbs and long face. A slim and tall body is matched with a delicate and pretty face. Slim and short statue is matched with a narrow but long face. With the exception of a few figures most are well and suitably arranged in basically correct proportion. We have gone over 617 clay figures and found that the proportion between various parts tallies in the main with oral instructions on proportions given by folk painters. These proportions are usually verbally handed down from generation to generation. To quote a few examples: A man may stand seven *chi* ($\frac{1}{3}$ metre) high. When he sits down the size becomes five. With his legs crossed the size becomes 3 and half *chi*. One shoulder is equal to three heads. One embrace equals to two faces. One face equals to five eyes. The face is equal to three foreheads. The palm is equal to half a face. One elbow equals to three fists. One's head is equal to one's foot in length.

In sculpturing details of the body the artists have paid attention to anatomical relations, such as the length of fingers and joints, the thickness of muscles, and the instep is described as high in the inside and low in the outside. All these are rationally sound. The corner of the eye is described as low in the inside and high on the outside. The upper eye lid covers the lower. Every detail is given by the artists about the nasal bone, the two cavities of the nose and the edge of the ear. The clay warriors are seen with rounded legs for a person who is standing and flattened legs for one in kneeling position. The corner of the lips become upward when one is laughing and the muscle between the eyebrows becomes a pimple or knot when a man gets angry. All these details are reasonable enough. Yet it has also been discovered that ten odd clay figures are disproportionately modelled, with either arms being too short or too long, or with one long arm and another arm short, or with feet too small or hands too big. This shows that the sculptors vary in their standard of artistic achivement. On the whole, the shape of

Qin clay figures is basically correct, save for a few which have short hands. The anatomy of clay figures is in keeping with reality. The clay figures give us a feeling that they are portraits of real persons.

The spirit and mettle of the soldiers and their outward appearances have been combined into an integral whole. It embodies the tradition of Chinese aesthetic standard which calls for concrete shape and vivid expression. The Qin sculpture has successfully mastered not only the entire work but also a description of details. In technique round sculpture, bas relief, and delineation by lines have been used together in an integral manner. The massive and three dimensional statues are done in round sculpture by means of embossment to represent the body, quantity and shape of images. In the case of adornment and dress details are executed by means of embossment, kneading and pasting. The result produced is incised relief. This is particularly effective for bringing out details. In the representation of torso or trunk what the artists have done is rather general. No muscles are represented on the whole. However, to bring out vividness the artists have included the major parts of the torso. To sculpture a man in smile the sculptor shows the muscle of the cheeks to tend a bit upward. The sculptor raises the muscle between eyebrows to show a man in anger. He tightens the triangular muscle behind the ears to show a man who is stretching his neck. Otherwise the muscle is relaxed and forms itself into a concave. On the whole the sculpture of the Qin clay figures is general rather than detailed. Yet details are also shown to emphasise certain expressions. Such minute executions nevertheless belong to or are subordinated to general descriptions.

3. Expressions on Warriors

An outstanding achievement of the Qin sculpture lies in the presentation of variegated protypes showing different status, age and distinguished features. In order to represent men in different status the sculptor pays attention to the delineation of dresses and adornments as well as revelation of looks and expressions. Different key __. sions are shown in different people. The general is represented as a man who is above others, marked by dignity and seriousness. This feature is common to all generals. In addition to this common trait the general may have certain individual traits, such as gentleness and stylishness experience and prudence. In some the sculptor seeks to show dignity and sturdiness. Middle-ranking and low grade officers are dressed in different suits from the generals. They also adopt different attitude and have diverse spiritual outlook. On the whole they show respect and care, scruples, bravery and experience. The general and his two aides unearthed from the No. 4 square in No. 2 pit are a case in point. Other officers standing in rows have bushy beard almost like horns plus a few whiskers to show straight forwardness and honesty of character. Some have wrinkles on the forehead to show their age and experience. These seem to indicate that the promotion of officers in the Qin army depended much on merits. It was necessary that the officers should display respectful attitude and loyalty. Even more variegated expressions are found among ordinary warriors. For instance, archers kneel with left leg. The right leg is placed horizontally on the ground. The body is slightly inclined to the left. The two hands are energetically pulling the bow. The eyes are directed to front left. The expression is one of vividness. The archer in standing position has been

17

captured during a moment when he is trying to shoot the arrow. He wears a genuine look. The archer is the exact replica of the one described in Spring and Autumn of Wu and Yu states, an early Chinese literature. According to this literature the archer places the left leg vertically and the right leg horizontally. The left hand looks like holding a branch. The right hand looks like holding a child. The archer shoots with the right hand, with the left hand still. The standing archer in the Qin Shi Huang's tumulus fits in exactly with this description. This means that the sculpture is modelled after real archers of the Qin Dynasty. Some archers are seen to be on the point of shooting the arrow. The two types are the only dynamic representations. For the most part the archers are still life representations, however.

The cavalry are another vividly portrayed sculptures. The cavalry holds the rein with one hand and a bow on the other to the front left of the head of the horse. The status is one of sturdiness and the expression one of bravery. The cavalry is the picture of strength and vigor as well as handsomeness. The horse seems to be neighing. The look of the high horse goes well with the vigor of the cavalry.

The drivers are sculptured at the moment when the chariot and horses are ready for the journey, with the driver holding the rein. It is a tense and concentrated moment. The two assistants hold the chariot with one hand and a long weapon in the other. The four horses drawing the chariot display an eargerness to go.

Even the rows and rows of foot soldiers all display evident characteristics. If we examine their countenances carefully. The modelling of clay horses has won great exclaim from many experts. In the delineation of clay figures of warriors some flaws may have been detected. But in the modelling of horses one can find consummation of art. The horses are sculptured exactly and vividly like real ones. The method of representation is one of concentration and conciseness. The head, the tail and the torso are shown to be full of muscles and strong bones. The four legs are conspicuously drawn with strong and straight lines and curves. The head is sculptured even more carefully, given a great many details. The sculpturing is excellent with due emphasis on certain things and leaving out the minor details. The face and cheeks seem to have been chipped with a knife. They show unusual conciseness. The eyelid, the two openings of the nose, and the mouth are finely carved with dark lines in detail. Shown under the light the horses display the high and the low, the light and the dark and a rich gradation. The sculptor has done wonders with the eyes, ears, nose, and mouth of the horses, which he portrays with forcefulness. The eye sockets are high. The eyes themselves are like bronze bells but rather bright. The ears prick forward. The mane is tossing and tail wagging. The horse is stretching its neck and neighing. This all the more brings out the expression. From an anatomical viewpoint all parts of clay horses have been correctly proportioned. Some experts maintain that it would be very hard to conceive that these horses had been sculptured more than 2,000 years ago, had it not been known that they indeed were.

On the whole the thousands of figures in the ancient grave of the first Qin emperor give one the impression that a batch of highly organised and highly disciplined and real warriors (together with their horses) are before us. They show the strict discipline of the Qin army, in which it was said that the brave was rewarded, the coward punished and sell-out executed. Yet a few figures among them seem to be out of place. Some lean and small and emanciated show suppressed emotion and dispirit. It was said that severe and hard labor, including forced military service had been imposed on the people during the first emperor's reign. The severe punishment meted out to those who disobeyed brought untold suffering to the people. From the legal code of the Qin Dynasty one sees many instances in which people had tried to dodge the harsh military service. The look on the emanciated soldiers is the expression of dissatisfaction and anger of the people. Though few in number the clay figures are much treasured as they are a reflection of the deep and sharpening social contradiction of the Qin Dynasty. They show the resistance of the people.

4. Colorings in Qin Sculpture

The clay figures of warriors and horses we see today in the Qin tumulus usually display a sort of dull green. This is the color of the clay itself. It is not painted color. The pottery had been originally painted fully. But they had become discolored due to fire and corrosion of water and earth after having been buried underground for over 2,000 years. Only a few traces of painted color now remain. Hardly a figure has retained its original painted color. From what has been discovered so far the following colors have been used: vermilion, red, purple, pink, deep green, light green, deep purple, blue, pale blue, yellow, organge yellow, black, white, redishness, etc. The dyes have been chemically analysed and known to contain mineral qualities. The clays were modelled at first, fired in the kiln and then dyed. The dyeing method calls for the application of gelatin as base. The color is then painted on the clay model. Color mixing agent also contains a rich quantity of gelatin. The color is then applied on the model. Most parts of the model have been dyed once. The face, hands and feet are, however, dyed twice.

What is the artistic effect achieved in painting colorful designs on terra cotta figures? We can get a general impression by going over the better preserved models, though it is impossible to see the original paintings as most of them have discolored. The driver and two assistants on the chariot in No. 1 test square of the No. 2 pit are good examples. The driver wears a green long jacket, on top of which an armor with bright red plates, white nails and vermilion belt. There is a pair of long light purple trousers. The puttees are green. Redish black shoes are matched with vermilion shoe strings. A white turban with vermilion hair belt can be seen on the head. The turban is covered with a redish long top with pale purple string. The face, hands and feet are painted in pink. His white eyes are coupled with black pupils. The eyebrows and beard are painted with lines drawn in black ink.

The assistant on the right wears a vermilion long coat, frilled in pale green. The short trousers are blue. A binding for the shank is redish purple. The color of the coat of mail, shoes and turban is the same as that of the driver. The assistant on the left wears a green long jacket, pale purple short trousers with puttee that is white on top and deep purple at the bottom. The color for other parts of the body is much the same as that of the other two persons. The cavalry unearthed in No. 12 square of the No. 2 pit wears a green coat with vermilion frills. The belt on the waist is redish. The pair of trousers is in light purple. The short boots are in redish color, with vermilion strings. The redish cap is painted all over with spotted plum designs. The color of the coat of mail is much the same. The general unearthed in the No. 9 square of the No. 2 pit wears a red inner jacket, a green coat on top plus vermilion long trousers and redish brown shoes and redish brown hat. The color of the coat of mail and the belt is perhaps most magnificent. There is an exquisite geometrical design in color at the back below the hair and the portion around it. On shoulders and the back are displayed eight colorful knots. As for the horse the body is usually red (like dried date), black mane and white horse shoes.

From the above description one gathers that the cloring on the Qin pottery figures is distinguished by lucidity and liveliness as well as a strong contrast in the application of colors to the objects. A red jacket is contrasted with green or pale purple or pale blue under wear. Green jacket is contrasted with red or pale purple trousers. Armor plates that are redish brown black are contrasted with white or vermilion armor mail and vermilion plate string. This results in a marked difference in color so that the atmosphere is one of warmth in the battle array, full of power and grandeur. The effect produced shows that if the eyes are sculptured small, then white is applied to the eye and black to the pupils to make the eyes very bright. The artist has combined scuplture with painting, producing a good artistic effect. Colors are applied on the plane surface of objects. The color itself does not show darkness or lightness nor changes in light and shade. Changes are shown only with the concave or convext parts of the body or lines in three dimensional modelling. Four clay horses in the No. 1 pit are, however, painted date-like red on the light side and deep green on the shaded side, such as the belly, the lower part of the neck, and the inside part of the limb. Although these are only a few cases they nevertheless show the artists are trying to achieve light and shade, high and low and changes in gradation by means of coloring. This has great significance in the history of sculpture.

The art of Qin clay sculpture has left us with a very deep impression. The figures are burial sacrifices in the first Qin emperor's grave. They are a microcosm of his army. On this account the principles of Qin artistic creation have been determined. The army, a weapon in the hands of the rising landlord class which took power is represented as something mighty and possessed with an awe-inspiring spirit. With this cardinal principle the artists have produced genuine and typical symbols of the real Qin army. Although the terra cotta figures have certain defect they play an epoch-making role.in serving as a link between the past and the future. The realistic style has much to do with the will of the ruling class, yet it has produced an artistic method that epitomises and refines. This method has been inherited by later generations. It has been evidently adopted by artists in sculpturing horses in the Han and Tang Dynasties. The art of the Qin sculpture has provided the first model in the history of ancient Chinese sculpture for later generations of artists to copy.

(Translated be He Fei)

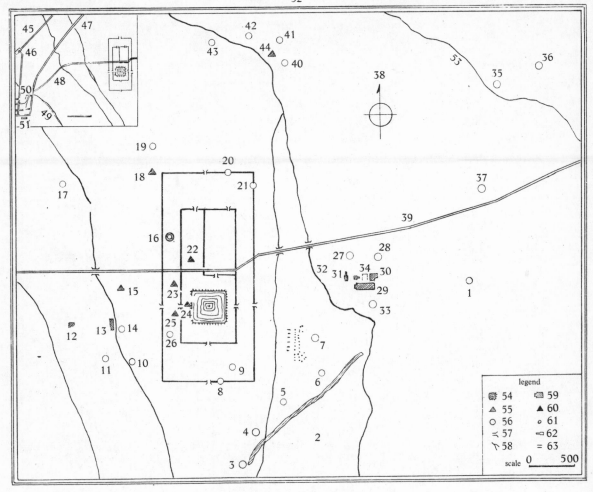

1 Shanrencun

2 Site of Wuling

3 Chenjiayao

4 Yangjia

5 Lijia

6 Dujia

7 Shangjiaocun

8 Shangchencun

9 Xiachencun

10 Dongjiagou

11 Yaochitou

12 Tombs of prisoners

13 Tombs of prisoners

14 Zhaobeihucun

15 Qin kiln

16 Yanzhai Commune

17 Zhuanfancun

18 Zhengzhuang remains

19 Zhengzhuangcun

20 Maojiacun

21 Xiajiaocun

22 Architectural remains

23 Architectural remains

24 Bronze chariot pit

25 Precious bird and beast pit

26 Yuejiagou

27 Xiahecun

28 Xiyangcun

29 No. 1

30 No. 2

31 No. 3

32 ancient tombs

33 Wangjiacun

34 Pit of pottery figures

35 Huzhaicun

36 Xihuangcun

37 Dongaicun

38 north

39 Lin-Ma Highway

40 Yuchicun

41 Wudongcun

42 Wuzhong

43 Wuxi

44 Site of Yuchi

45 Long-Hai Railway

46 railways station

47 Xi-Tong Highway

48 Lin-Ma Highway

49 Fengwang River

50 Lintong

51 Huaqing Pool

52 Sketch Map of the Mausoleum of Qin Shi Huang and Pit of Terra-cotta Figures

53 Youchuan River

54 rammed earth

55 sites

56 village

57 entrance

58 river

59 pit of warrior

60 pit of horse shed

61 pit of knelling figures

62 attendant pit

63 highway

Bronze four-horse chariot

team No. 2 renovated

In December 1980, at the west flank of the tomb of the First Emperor of Qin, near Xi'an, two groups of huge bronze chariots, bronze men and bronze horses have been formed. Each group consists of one chariot, four horses and one man. The two groups were placed in marching order, one after another in a line toward the west. All are half life-size drivers and horses. The two chariots are completely equipped and conspicuously decorated. This is another important find after the discovery of the terracotta figures at the mausoleum's east side in 1974.

The bronze four-horse chariots are burial objects in Qinshihuang Mausoleum. Judging from the luxurious and exquisite head-dress and decorations, these bronze chariots, bronze men and bronze horses were designed after the chariots of Qin queen, imperial conqubine or crown prince. They will be invaluable to specialists in history, metallurgy, fine arts and other fields.

View of the First Emperor's Mausoleum

Distant View of the Museum of the Terra-cotta Army of Qin Shi Huang

An External Shot of the Museum of the Terra-cotta Army of Qin Shi Huáng

View of Pit No.

Column in Trench No. 4-8 in
the East of the Pit (back)

Column on Southern Side in the East of the Pit

Column of Vanguards in the East of the Pit

Column of Vanguards in the East of the Pit

Column of War-
riors in the Cen-
tral Part in the
East of the Pit

Procession Scene on the Northern Side in the East of the Pit

Procession Scene on the Northern Side in the East of the Pit

Warriors Dressed in Armour

Procession Scene (Horses, Warriors in Armour, Infantrymen)

Pottery Figures of Infantrymen

Pottery Figures of Warriors and Horses

Pottery Figures of Horses and
Warriors in Armour

Procession Scene in Trench No. 5, 6
in the East of Pit (back)

Procession Scene in Trench No. 7, 8
in the Center in the East of Pit

Procession Scene in Trench No. 4 in the East of Pit

Pottery Infantrymen and Horses Drawing Chariots

Detail: Head of Pottery Horse

Pottery Figures in the East of Pit (looking from south to north)

Column of Vanguards in the East of Pit (looking from north to south)

Pottery Horses and Track of Chariot

Series of Marks Left by the Chariots

Pottery Figure of a General

Detail: Head of a General

Pottery Figure of a General (looking from behind)

Pottery Figure of a General (detail)

Detail: Head of a Cavalryman's Pommelled Horse (Pit No. 2)

Cavalryman and Pommelled Horse (detail)

Detail: Head of Figure of a Cavalryman (side view)

Pottery Figure of a Cavalryman (profile)

Pottery Figures of a Cavalryman and Pommelled Horse

Head of Pottery Figure of a General (profile)

Pottery Figure of a General (profile)

Pottery Figure of a General

Detail: Head of Pottery Figure of a General

Detail: Head of Pottery Figure of a
Kneeling Archer (Pit No. 2)

Pottery Figure of a Kneeling Archer (profile)

Pottery Figure of a Kneeling Archer

Pottery Figure of a Kneeling Archer
(looking from behind)

Detail: Head of Figure of a General (Profile, Pit No. 2)

Pottery Figure of a General (Pit No. 2)

Pottery Figure of a Warrior (Pit No. 2)

Detail: Head of Pottery Figure of a Warrior

Pottery Figure of a Warrior Shooting
from a Standing Position (detail)

Pottery Figure of a Warrior Shooting from a
Standing Position (looking from behind)

Detail: Head of Pottery Figure of a Warrior
Shooting from a Standing Position

Pottery Figure of a Warrior Shooting
from a Standing Position

Detail: Head of Figure of a Robed Warrior

Pottery Figure of a Robed Warrior

Pottery Figures of Infantry Group

Detail: Head of Pottery Figure of a Robed Warrior

Pottery Figure of Robed Warior (detail)

Detail: Head of Pottery Figure of a
Robed Warrior

Pottery Figures of Vanguards at the
Southeast End of the Pit

Pottery Figures at the Southeast End of the Pit

Detail: Head of Pottery Figure of a Robed Warrior

Pottery Figures of Warriors at the
Center in the East of the Pit

Pottery Figure
of Officers

Pottery Officers, Drivers and Infantrymen

Detail: Head of Pottery Figure of an Officer

Pottery Figure of an Officer (detail)

Pottery Attendants and Infantrymen

Pottery Attendants and Infantrymen

Pottery Figures of Infantrymen
(looking from behind)

Pottery Figures of Warriors Dressed
in Armours (Restoring Room)

Detail: Head of Pottery Figure of a Warrior
Dressed in Armour (Restoring Room)

Head of Pottery Figure of a
Warrior in Armour

Pottery Figures of Warriors Dressed in Armours

Pottery Figures of Warrior Dressed
in Armours (Restoring Room)

Pottery Figures of Warriors
Dressed in Armours

Pottery Figures of Warriors
Dressed in Armours

Detail: Head of Pottery Figure of a
Warrior Dressed in Armour (profile)

Detail: Head of Pottery Figure of a Warrior Dressed in Armour

Pottery Figure of a Horse (Pit No. 2)

Pottery Figure of a Horse

Detail: Head of Pottery Figure of a Horse

Pottery Figures of Horses

Pottery Figures under Excavation

Pottery Figures under Excavation

Pottery Figures under Excavation

Pottery Figures under Excavation

Pottery Figures under Excavation

Pottery Figures under Excavation

Pottery Figures under Excavation

Pottery Figures under Excavation

Pit Bottom Paved with Bricks

Traces of the Groove of Wood Used for Sealing Pit Door

Pottery Figures of Warriors being Excavated

Brick Wall of Pit

Pottery Figures of Warriors being Excavated

Pottery Figures of Warriors
being Excavated

Pottery Figures of Horses
being Excavated

Dress of a General
(back view)

Dress of a General

Detail: Hands of a General

Detail: Hat of a General   Dress of a General (profile)

Dress of a General (profile)   Dress of a General (back view)

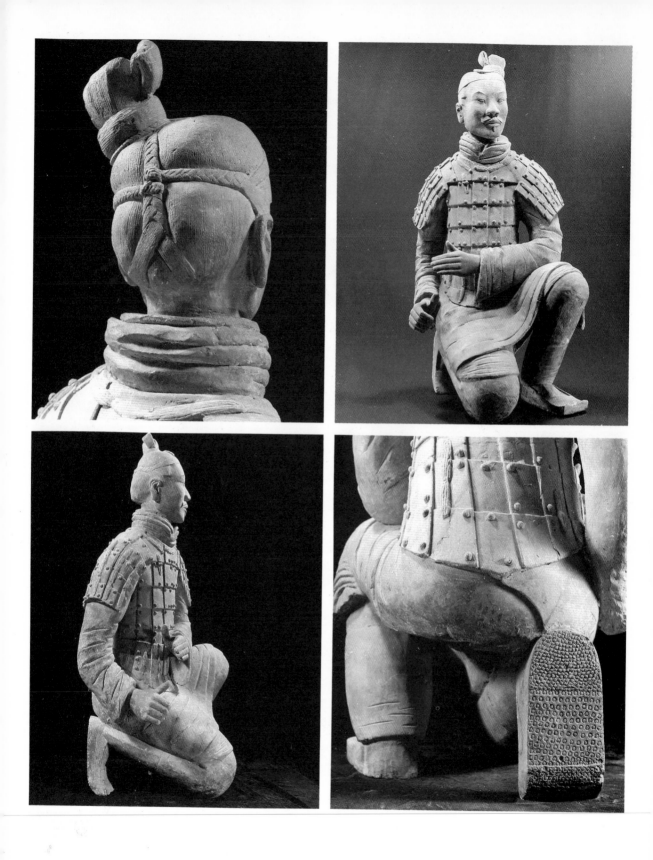

Kneeling Archer's Hair Worn in a Bun

Dress of a Kneeling Archer (profile)

Dress of a Kneeling Archer (front view)

Sole of the Shoe of a Pottery Figure

Hat Ornament and Hair Style   Dress of a Cavalrysoldier

Shoes of a Cavalrysoldier   Hat of a Cavalrysoldier

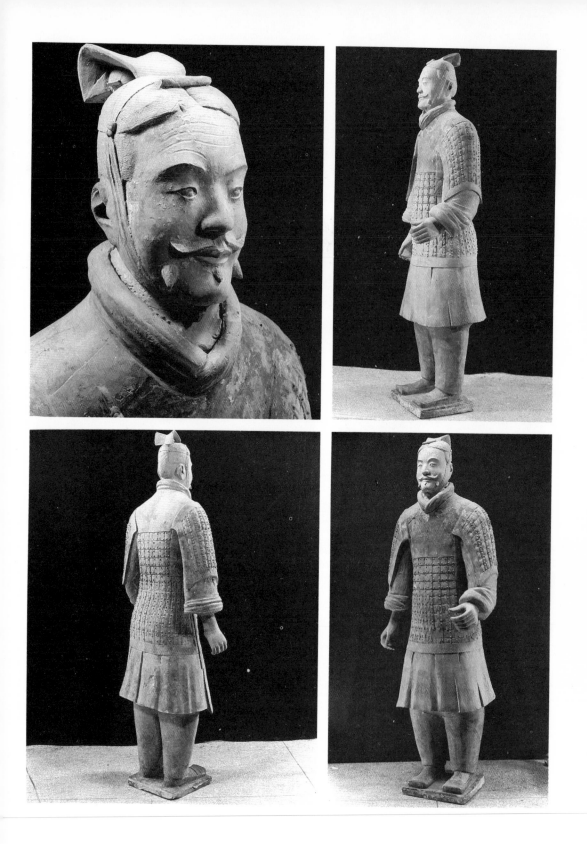

Hat of an Officer

Dress of an Officer (profile)

Dress of an Officer (back)

Dress of an Officer

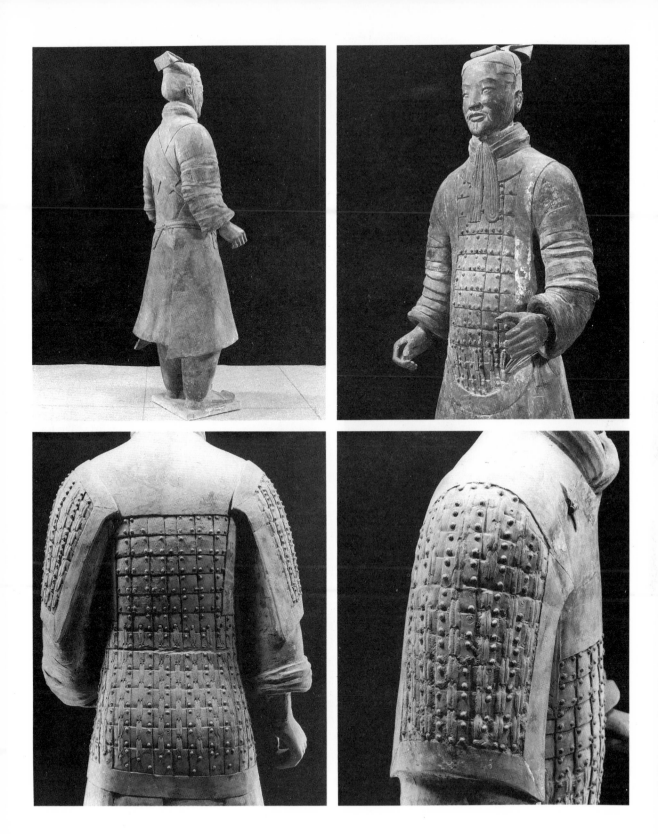

Cuirass (profile)   Cuirass (front)

Cuirass with Belt (back)   Cuirass (profile)

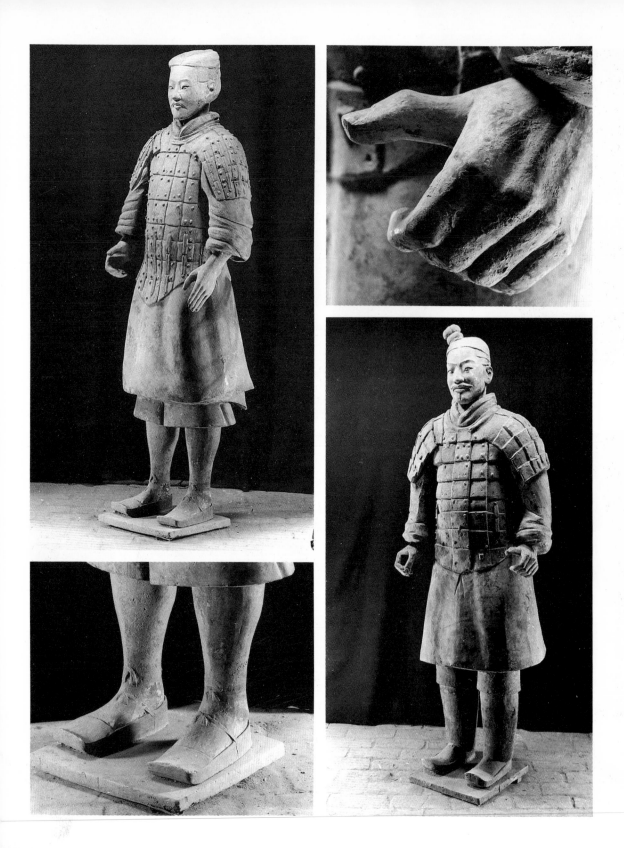

Dress of a Warrior in Armour   Hand of a Warrior in Armour

Shoes of a Warrior in Armour   Dress of a Warrior in Armour

Detail of Belt with Belt Hook

Detail of Collars of Underclothes and Coat

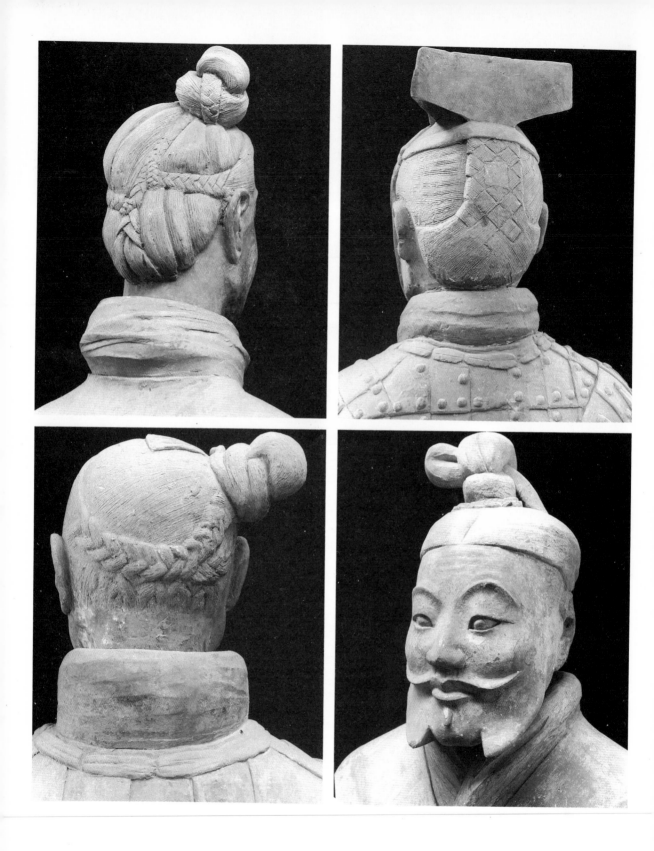

Detail of Coiffure and Facial Expression of Pottery Figure (1)

Detail of Coiffure and Facial Expression of Pottery Figure (2)

Detail of Coiffure and Facial Expression of Pottery Figure (3)

Detail of Coiffure and Facial Expression of Pottery Figure(4)

Detail of Coiffure and Facial Expression of Pottery Figure(5)

Detail of Coiffure and Facial Expression of Pottery Figure(6)

Bronze Dagger-axe

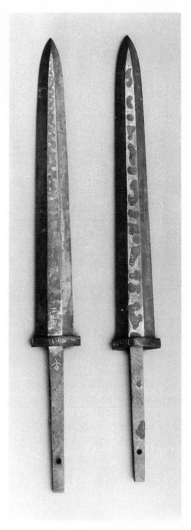

Bronze *pi*

Bronze Bat-
tle Axe

Bronze Spear

Detail of Coiffure and Facial Expression of Pottery Figure (6)

Bronze Dagger-axe

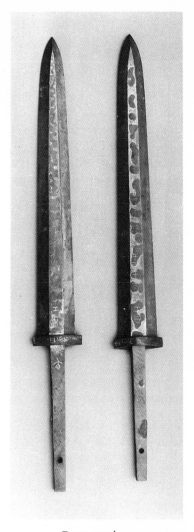

Bronze *pi*

Bronze Bat-
tle Axe

Bronze Spear

Bronze Crossbow

Inscriptions on Pottery Figure

Inscriptions on Pottery Figure

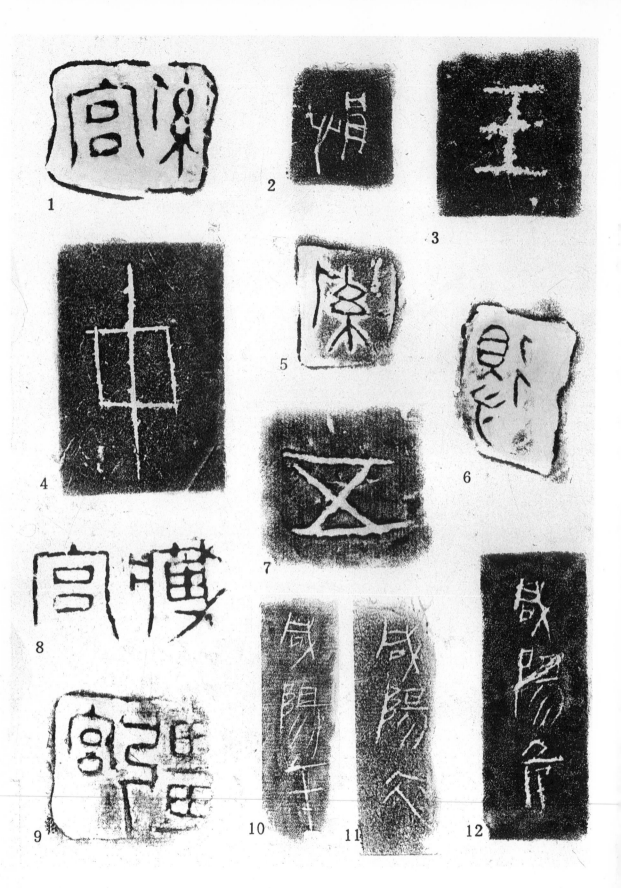

Rubbings from Pottery Figures